Squirrel bought a birthday gift for Little Bunny and ask

"Wrong, guess again."

"A round cake?"

Haha, this hat is just the right size.

Hmm, this beret is nice, but it's too small.

Little Bunny went to the shop to buy a hat. She spotted a lotus-leaf hat, tried it on, and found it was way too big.